CHECKMATE

CHECKMATE

Beat the Myths and Win the Game

JERRY L. SMITH

ARCHWAY
PUBLISHING

Archway Publishing books may be ordered through booksellers or by contacting:

Archway Publishing
1663 Liberty Drive
Bloomington, IN 47403
www.archwaypublishing.com
1 (888) 242-5904

Because of the dynamic nature of the Internet, any web addresses or links contained in this book may have changed since publication and may no longer be valid. The views expressed in this work are solely those of the author and do not necessarily reflect the views of the publisher, and the publisher hereby disclaims any responsibility for them.

Any people depicted in stock imagery provided by Getty Images are models, and such images are being used for illustrative purposes only. Certain stock imagery © Getty Images.

ISBN: 978-1-4808-6267-8 (sc)
ISBN: 978-1-4808-6268-5 (hc)
ISBN: 978-1-4808-6266-1 (e)

Library of Congress Control Number: 2018947591

Print information available on the last page.

Archway Publishing rev. date: 9/13/2018

CONTENTS

INTRODUCTION

SELLING INSURANCE is much different from selling a car, boat, house, or any other tangible item. The consumer cannot see, touch, or smell the insurance product. It requires greater sales skills to sell an intangible item. If you want to excel in a sales career, you need to have a strategic plan. Sure, you can make a substantial amount of money immediately. However, the real question is, how well do you perform over the long haul? Building a successful insurance sales career is not a sprint; it is a marathon.

Many insurance agents come out of the gate very strong. When I refer to "coming out of the gate," I am talking about the first five years of an agent's career. It is the second part of the race when they often become winded or burnt out. However, that second half is what really matters. This part of the race is where they need to excel. They have gained knowledge and experience, and the time has come to utilize it. The problem is that most agents don't have a strategic plan for the second half of the race. Their plan is to run the second half exactly the same way they ran the first half.

How many times have you heard someone say that at one point in their life they sold insurance for several years but that it just wasn't for them? Usually, they imply that their moral standards were too high for the job. The truth of the matter is that they just couldn't make it through the second half of the race.

Remember there are no good excuses for failure. Failure is failure. Our culture only remembers the winners, not the losers. Therefore, the key is to have a strategic plan for the second half of the race. How do you do that? Simple—have a really great plan for the beginning of the race. Invest in yourself. Focus on getting better every day. Grab knowledge everywhere you can. Just make sure the person you are grabbing it from actually knows what he or she is talking about. Then analyze and prepare your strategy for the second half of the race. Most importantly, follow through with the plan.

Recently, while I was on vacation with my wife and some friends in Saint Barthélemy, I received a phone call from a gentleman named Devin who had previously booked me to conduct a sales training seminar for a group of agents. After the seminar, Devin and I had a lengthy conversation about sales training, and he asked me if I would mind giving him my personal phone number. I jokingly replied that I would give him the number but that he should keep in mind that this number was for emergencies only.

So, there I was on vacation when my phone rang, and it was Devin. Just as I was about to answer the phone, my wife looked at me and said, "I hope that is an emergency." However, this was not because she was upset but because years ago while we were on a family vacation I'd told her that I would contribute to her shopping fund for every business call I handled on the trip. In her mind, this became a lifetime contract, and she has held me to it ever since.

Devin started the conversation by apologizing for contacting me on my personal line and stated that he had somewhat of an emergency. He explained to me that one of his agents, John, was on the verge of a sales breakdown. He stated that John had been an insurance agent for years and that he was depressed because he had never reached the level of success he had hoped for.

Devin said he considered John to be one of his closest friends and wanted to do something to help him. Devin was afraid that John would just give up on his insurance career. He asked me if I could possibly give his friend a call and try to help him.

I told him that I would give John a call, if he thought it would help. After I hung up with Devin, I took a moment to think about what he had told me. I tried to envision how John must be feeling and what may have caused it. I then proceeded to dial John's phone number.

When John answered the phone, I introduced myself. I explained to John that Devin had asked me, as a favor, to give him a call personally. I told him I wanted to take just a few minutes to find out if there was a way I could possibly help him elevate his sales.

All I had to do was crack the door, and John kicked it in. He burst into a conversation with a theme based on "the world is caving in" and "I have fallen and can't get up." The emotions just poured out of John. At one point, I was concerned that he might pass out from not taking a breath between sentences.

As I would try to interject something into the conversation, John just kept talking. I finally got him to stop and take a breath, and then I asked, "John, would you mind if I asked just a few questions so that I can get a better understanding of your situation?"

He replied, "No." I told him I had three questions I needed to ask. I asked him to tell me what he thought was the one thing that could have changed his career. He replied, "It was the leads, Jerry. I just never had access to really good leads."

I reminded him that earlier in our conversation he had told me that his entire career had been based around one product line, so I asked him, "What is your reason for not cross-selling other products?"

This question again opened the floodgates, as John gave me reason after reason justifying his sales mentality. He would say, "You can't do this, because of that." You have to do this. You can't do this. To be successful, you have to do it this way.

As my head was about to explode with John's continuous rambling about things that made absolutely no sense to me, I interrupted him and said, "John, I am sorry. I lied to you." He then stopped, in a state of total shock, and was totally silent. I said, "Yes, John, I lied to you. I told you that I only needed to ask you three questions. I now realize that I am going to need an additional question. Are you all right with that?"

He replied, "Yes."

I then asked John, "How did you come up with all these notions and rules about selling insurance?"

John replied, "Jerry, I was taught all this when I first started in insurance. I was fortunate enough to have some really good sales trainers."

Suddenly, it came to me: John had based his entire sales career on a series of sales myths taught to him by other people who believed in those same myths. He had spent years trying to find the mythical yellow brick road. His problem was that these rules and theories were just sales folklore, similar to urban legends. The only place these rules and theories actually existed was in the minds of salespeople who just didn't know any better.

I told John I believed I could help him. I explained to him that I just needed to ask him one last question. "John, could you tell me what you feel is the easiest way for you to learn something new?"

He replied, "I am a reader. That is how I like to learn new things."

So, I told John I had a solution for him and I would send it to him as soon as I got back from my vacation.

As I hung up from that conversation with John, I took a few moments to make some notes. While making those notes, it became apparent that there were ten different sales myths John believed in.

As I spent that time in Saint Barthélemy, I would take my spare time—or, in other words, the time when my wife was at the spa or pool—to write this booklet for John. As I finished it, I decided I wanted to share it with everyone. I wanted to free everyone from the chains of these sales myths that hold so many great insurance agents hostage.

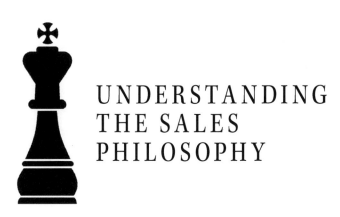

UNDERSTANDING THE SALES PHILOSOPHY

I N   O R D E R   to understand the philosophy behind this booklet, you need to have access to the details of my life that formed my sales philosophy. It is the foundation on which JLS Sales Academy was built. This is not a philosophy built around charisma, charm, personality, or sales talent. It is a template that can be easily replicated by any agent, regardless of his or her experience or skill set.

First of all, I will tell you that I had absolutely no desire during my younger years to become a salesperson. I grew up in Kokomo, Indiana. It was an automotive-industry-driven city. In 1963, I was adopted by a single woman who took me in and made me her world. My mother was a babysitter by trade. Being adopted provided me with a wonderful mother and an exceptional childhood. All the children my mother cared for became like siblings to me. My mother taught me to always believe in myself and others. She indoctrinated me into believing that I could accomplish anything that I set my mind to.

We lived very modestly. My mother could not afford a car, so we walked everywhere. I understood the difference between having and not having money at a very early age. Each week, I would walk to the grocery store with my mother, where we would buy food for the two of us and all the children she cared for. The decision-making process at the grocery store was easy: buy everything on sale! We shopped based not on what we wanted but on what we could get the most of for the least amount of money.

When I was about ten, I started playing chess. My best friend growing up also played chess. I started playing on the school chess team when I was in the sixth grade. I helped my school win numerous events and traveled throughout the Midwest to play in chess tournaments.

The problem was these events had entrance fees and there was an expense to attending them. I realized that I needed a way to make money. I decided to get a job delivering newspapers in order to make extra money and support my chess addiction. I saved whatever money I made—that wasn't spent on chess tournaments—to buy a moped. That moped enabled me to deliver even more newspapers in a shorter time. It provided me with a way to expand my newspaper route and make even more money.

Several of the kids in my neighborhood wanted to ride my moped. I would agree to let them ride it—with one condition: they had to help me deliver the newspapers that day. I then saved additional money to buy a second moped. I could deliver even more newspapers because my friends rode my second moped in exchange for delivering newspapers.

This was the point in my life when I discovered the importance of planning for the second half of the race. You see, I did not take into account that my friends would become bored with riding my mopeds or that their parents might buy them their own. I did not think through the fact that my route was too big for one person. So, as you might expect, I eventually sold one of the mopeds and scaled back the size of my newspaper route.

Throughout my high school years, I continued to play in chess tournaments. After graduating, I applied for admission to Indiana University. This is where my life as an insurance agent began. In 1983, while attending college, I was recruited to sell nursing home insurance and Medicare Supplement policies.

The pitch was simple: "Go get your insurance license, and we will teach you everything you need to know." They made it sound like money would start falling from the sky. You can make buckets of extra money part-time while you are in school. It sounded good, so I began to study and prepare for the licensing exam.

After getting my license, it was time to get my sales training. My sales trainer was a gentleman named Bob. He was as polished and smooth as it could get. Bob informed me that I needed to set aside three whole days to train with him. He said, "Clear your calendar, kid. I am going to show you how to make some real money!"

That first day with Bob was amazing. He sold deal after deal. He made the whole process look simple. At the end of the day, Bob asked me, "What do you think?"

I told him he certainly made it look easy.

The following morning, I woke up and prepared for my second day with Bob. During that day, I began to watch Bob's mannerisms and how he carried himself. I watched how he communicated with people. Again, Bob sold numerous deals. Selling was just second nature to him. To say that he was charismatic was an understatement!

The third morning, Bob informed me that we would not be going into the field that day. He told me we would just go to breakfast and talk about my future. As we sat there waiting for our food, Bob asked me what I thought about the last few days. I told him it was an eye-opening experience and that watching him work was truly amazing.

During breakfast, he continued to explain how this was the perfect opportunity for me. I could go to school and make a lot of money working part-time. I might eventually decide to make selling insurance my career. He explained how it gave me options.

After breakfast, Bob gave one of the most serious looks that I had ever seen and said, "Are you ready to change your life?"

At that point, being put totally on the spot, I replied, "No."

Bob, appearing confused, asked me, "Why?"

I told him that I just did not feel a sales job was for me. I explained that I was very impressed with him but that it just did not feel like I had the same smooth, charismatic personality he had. I told him I really appreciated the time he had spent with me but that I was going to look for a different solution. I then proclaimed I just did not have the personality required for the job.

Bob was silent as we got back in his car. As he drove me back to my car, I could tell he was in a deep state of thought. It was either that or a state of extreme disappointment in me; I wasn't sure which. I do know it was the quietest he had been in the last three days.

As we arrived at my car, Bob turned to me and said, "Jerry, over the last few days, I have come to realize that you are a very intelligent young man." He then explained to me that selling is not always about personality. Just because he was a charismatic salesperson and his method of selling was based on personality did not mean I had to be like him to be successful.

At that point, he made a statement that changed my life forever. He said, "Jerry, I believe if you took the time to analyze the sales process just like you do a game of chess, you could be good at this business. Maybe even better than I am."

He then asked me if I would do him a favor and think for a day about what he had told me. I agreed to ride with him one last time, two days later.

The following morning, I started to break down everything I had watched Bob do. I spent the entire day thinking, reflecting, and analyzing each of Bob's presentations. I broke each presentation down and looked at it as a systematic process. I analyzed how he got each person to proceed with the application and write a check. I thought about how he phrased things and answered questions.

I took out a pad of paper and started mapping out the process. I wanted to create a strategy based upon a structured process instead of sales skill. I mapped out probable consumer questions and determined how I would respond to them. I also mapped out questions that I might ask a consumer and their possible responses.

Before I realized, it was dark outside. By ten o'clock that evening, and about fifty pages of notes later, I had finished developing and analyzing a sales process.

The following morning, I met with Bob. When I got into his car, he looked at me and said, "Today, we are going to do something different." He pulled up to the restaurant where we had been eating breakfast each day and then told me he was going in for breakfast—and I was not.

He then handed me an index card with the name "Martha Jones" and an address on it and told me he wanted me to drive to her house and tell her she needed to buy nursing home insurance. He said, "Just use my sales kit. It is in the back seat."

I watched Bob enter the restaurant. I wasn't sure how I felt about this. Part of me was nervous, and part of me was excited. The excited part was because I would actually get to test my strategy. I told myself, "It is just like playing a game of chess." However, in this case if I win the customer wins too.

As I arrived at my destination, I reminded myself to stay calm and focused. I got out of the car and proceeded to the door. I knocked on Martha's door, and as I stood there, the nervous side of me started to creep back in. I started to hope that Martha was not home. But suddenly, the door opened, and I was face-to-face with Martha. After a brief conversation, Martha invited me into her home.

Meanwhile, Bob was eating breakfast and flirting with the waitress. He loved flirting with one particular waitress. He had informed me days earlier that he was going to get her to ask him on a date. I had asked him one morning why he didn't just ask her out. He said that there was no challenge in that. He stated that the challenge was to get her to ask *him* out.

As Bob finished his breakfast, he wondered how I was doing. He expected me back at any time. He hoped that I at least would get a chance to talk to Martha. He started to prepare for his pep talk. He knew I would come back all beaten up and bruised. His job was to pick me up and dust me off. He would give me the "tough part is over" talk.

Another hour passed, and Bob was still waiting for me. He started to get concerned. It dawned on him that he had just given this young kid the keys to his brand-new convertible Chrysler LeBaron. Did I get in an accident? Was I just out driving around?

Another hour passed, and Bob was definitely in panic mode. He was just about ready to lose his mind. All of a sudden, he saw me walk through the door of the restaurant. As I walked up to him, I could tell he was concerned. He asked me if I had gotten into a car accident! I replied, "No."

I could tell that he was relieved as he responded, "That's good."

I then reached over and placed a check down on the counter in front of him that was made out to United Equitable for $1,182 and said, "But I did pick this up."

That was the start of my career in insurance. I sold the first call and then just kept selling. I continued to refine and analyze my sales process, as if it was a game of chess. About nine months later, I left Indiana University and started a full-time insurance career. It was the second and last job of my life.

As a personal producer, I have made millions of dollars throughout my career. I have attended insurance-producer conventions all over the world and created a process that averages over $40,000 in commission per sale. Now, I want to share this process with you and provide you with all the details, so you can do it too. The training we provide through JLS Sales Academy can provide you with a systematic, duplicable template for success.

It is common for agents to develop some bad habits or beliefs throughout their careers. Often, those habits and beliefs start at the very beginning of the career. That is why it is often said that it is easier to train a new agent than to attempt to fix an old one. I personally believe that experienced agents can learn to change; it just requires effort. The key is to identify where the problem exists. Is it bad habits, lack of knowledge, or belief in sales myths? All these can be detrimental to an agent's career.

Here are the ten myths that I identified during my conversation with John that affected his career:

1) Be great at selling your product.
2) You need good leads.
3) Cross-selling is difficult.
4) Fact-finding is easy.
5) Warm up and then jump into the presentation.
6) Presentation materials are for amateurs.
7) Great salespeople can wing it.
8) Don't present multiple products simultaneously.
9) Lead generation is difficult.
10) Closing the sale is difficult.

As we take a closer look at the sales myths that have put a stranglehold on John's career, remember that there is always a way to fix everything. You deserve to have the career you have always dreamed of. The only person who can keep you from achieving it is yourself.

I want you to remember one very important thing and this out of all things tends to be the hardest thing for agents to understand.

> *"The most difficult hurdles to overcome are the self-imposed limitations that we place upon ourselves!"*
> —JERRY L. SMITH

MYTH 1

You Must Be Great at Selling Your Product

T H E   M Y T H that often creates the biggest downfall of insurance agents is the belief that they need to be great at selling their product.

So, what are we talking about when we refer to being great at selling their product? Why is that a bad thing? First, let's take a look at the sales philosophies of insurance agents who are great at selling their product.

These agents typically sell based on one of two strategies, which revolve around either price or product features. The most prevalent method is based upon price. The agents will position their ability to access pricing information on multiple plans as their value to the consumer.

Selling based on price is the lowest of all sales skill sets. Actually, it does not require a sales skill set at all. Usually, there is little to no focus on creating a need. The agent is simply positioning him- or herself as a professional price shopper for a product where the need is already established.

What happens when another agent contacts their client with a lower-priced product? Often, their client will go with the new agent. After all, isn't that how the agent convinced them to become their client to begin with? They showed the client a lower-cost plan and convinced them that they should be more concerned about the cost versus the insurance company or agent.

This type of agent is always chasing prices. Every time a new company enters the market, or an insurance carrier adjusts their pricing, this agent wants to get contracted with that company. These agents fear that if they do not have the lowest price to offer their clients, their clients will go elsewhere.

This creates a cycle of constant "price shopping." The agent often spends more time shopping prices for his or her existing clients than focusing on obtaining new clients.

The problem with this sales philosophy is that technology is changing the world. The fundamental value that this sales philosophy provides is access to pricing information. However, today this information can be easily obtained. Using the internet to research pricing is not complex. Many consumers view it as a much simpler process than meeting with an agent.

There are three obstacles that the price-shopping agent will face in the future. The first I refer to as the "Wal-Mart Effect." The concept of insurance superstores on the internet has already started. The ability to go to one place and research the rates of numerous carriers is already here. Smaller agents and agencies will not be able to compete against the large wholesalers and insurance carriers in this marketplace.

Today, the internet is dominated with lead-capture sites. These sites are in the business of capturing and then selling leads to insurance carriers and agents. However, it is only a matter of time before the lead-generation business takes a back seat to internet enrollments.

The second obstacle I refer to as the "Progressive Effect." We have all been a witness to the dominance of internet enrollments in the casualty-insurance industry. Consumers enrolling online because of lower premiums is a growing trend.

Agents struggle to compete against internet pricing. Often, the companies they represent offer consumers lower prices online than the agent can offer the consumer for the exact same company. It is only a matter of time before insurance carriers in the senior market develop successful direct-to-consumer marketing strategies for price-driven products, like Medicare Supplement plans.

The third obstacle I refer to as the "Blockbuster Effect." Many of us can remember the days of renting a movie at the local video store. We also remember our excitement as the superstore of video rental came to our area, and Blockbuster changed the landscape for video rental. Soon, small video stores began to fail, because they could not compete with Blockbuster.

Then the market changed again with Redbox and Netflix. You could get DVD rentals mailed directly to your home. There was no longer a need for a brick-and-mortar location for renting videos. Eventually, the post office was replaced with the internet for delivery of video rentals.

There is an entire generation of people who have never been in a Blockbuster store. They have never rented a movie and then received it through the mail. The senior insurance market will change in a similar way. People aging into the senior market have more choices and access to information than ever before. Their ability to compare plan features and rates is right at their fingertips.

The agents who base their sales strategy on a purely price-driven philosophy will end up just like a Blockbuster Video store in the future, because their service and method of delivery will become outdated.

Now that we have discussed the pitfalls of implementing a sales strategy based purely upon price, I want to discuss the second sales strategy, which is based upon product features. This sales strategy requires a higher level of sales skill than that of a price-driven sales strategy. After all, the agent must create a need or problem that can be eliminated or reduced with benefits offered by his or her product.

These agents are well versed on the advantages and benefits their product provides. They study the competition and know their product's strong points. The ability to demonstrate the need and benefits of their product is second nature.

This sales strategy focuses solely on the product itself and the functionality of each provision, rider, and benefit. It is a sales mentality based upon getting to the point, creating the need, and closing the sale. A comprehensive fact-finding process is typically not a focal point for this style of presentation. Agents who embrace this sales strategy usually focus on one product line and have a very limited skill set when it comes to selling across multiple product lines.

So here is what we know. Agents who sell based solely upon price, product features, or a combination of both can be great at selling their product. But is being great at selling your product good enough? Will it provide you with the level of success you deserve?

To demonstrate my point, I want to introduce you to three different insurance agents: Randy, Paul, and John. They all work in the senior health insurance market. For our example, we are going to say that all three agents are going to make a presentation to the same prospective client, Janet Smith, who currently is enrolled in original Medicare and carries a Medicare Supplement policy.

Randy is a successful insurance agent and feels that he is an expert in Medicare Supplemental coverage. His sales strategy is based upon comparing premiums with a focus on saving people money on their Medicare Supplement premiums. Randy wants to show Janet that he is a professional shopper and that with his expertise, he can save her a few hundred dollars a year on her Medicare Supplement premiums. His fact-finding process is nonexistent. The only two facts that really matter for his presentation are Janet's current premium and that she is insurable. His presentation will be relatively short and to the point. Randy is very good at selling Medicare Supplement plans and hopes to make about $300 by selling Janet a new Medicare Supplement plan.

Paul's sales strategy is based upon product features and his product of choice is nursing home coverage. Paul is well versed on the shortfalls in Medicare coverage with regard to nursing home confinement. He understands that many people would rather recuperate at home than in a nursing home. His product offers benefits for nursing home care and home health care. Paul's sales strategy will be based upon immediately creating the need for his product. The fact-finding process will be a very surface-oriented approach and will not drill down deeply into the circumstances of Janet's lifestyle and finances. Paul's sales mentality is based more on showing Janet certain facts and statistics instead of uncovering the intricate details of Janet's circumstances. He wants to show Janet how she can protect herself from the costs of a nursing home confinement. Paul hopes to sell Janet a nursing home policy that will earn him a commission of about $1,500.

John's sales strategy is based upon concepts. His presentation will not be based upon saving money or product features. He is going to talk to Janet about the process of aging and her ability to live out the rest of her life the way she is currently accustomed to, on her own terms. John is going to implement a more in-depth fact-finding process. John wants to know about Janet's finances and her concerns about sickness, death, and her children. He wants a full understanding of her current and past health conditions and her expectations regarding her current and future lifestyle.

John is going to explain to Janet that as people age, their health will eventually deteriorate. Often, this means we have to go to the hospital. When a person enters the hospital, he or she will eventually leave the hospital and go home, go to a nursing home, or end up at a funeral home. He will explain to Janet that those are the three places that a person should have some kind of plan for.

Having the ability to live out the rest of her life based on her terms and the lifestyle she is currently accustomed to should be the ultimate goal. John's presentation will be based on the concept of creating a road map for that goal.

Janet doesn't want to get sick or go to the hospital. However, if she does, she does not want to be left with a major out-of-pocket expense. If Janet needs recuperative care, she would like to get it at home if possible. But can she financially afford to get the care at home? She would like to live out the rest of her life in the comfort of her own home, but what happens if she needs physical assistance in order to stay in her home?

The last place Janet wants to go is the nursing home. If she doesn't have a choice, how will she pay the bill? Janet understands that everyone will eventually die, and she does not want her funeral expenses to be a financial burden on her children.

John will ask Janet these questions: "Janet, what would you say if I told you I could show you an affordable plan that would pay your doctors and hospital bills, in addition to paying for care at home or in a nursing home and would pay for your funeral?" He would say, "Janet, if you could eliminate all those problems and give you the ability to live out the rest of your life on your own terms based on the lifestyle you are currently accustomed to, would that make sense to you? Would you feel better knowing that regardless of what the circumstances were, you had a plan?"

John will sell Janet a Medicare Supplement, nursing home policy with a home health care rider and a final-expense policy all at the same time. His presentation was based on the concept of Janet being able to live out the rest of her life the way she is currently accustomed to and on her own terms.

A presentation based on a concept is far more compelling than a presentation based on an individual product or a price comparison. John's product is the freedom to live life without worry; to know that there is always a plan. Can you really put a price tag on that?

His commission on the sale is about $3,000. The commission is ten times higher than Randy's and doubles Paul's. Even though Randy and Paul are both great at selling their product, in the end, being great at selling your product just won't get you where you need to go.

The ability to sell concepts is where the truly talented sales-people reside. If you want to keep living in the house of above average, just continue to be great at selling your product. If you want to take your skills to the next level, learn to sell concepts versus product.

MYTH 2

You Need Good Leads

IN MY OPINION, the sales process is just that: a process. It is something you can strategically control, to improve your performance and efficiency.

By utilizing customer analysis, strategic positioning, and personal development, you can sell in any situation you encounter in the senior market. So, what does any of this have to do with needing good leads?

Often, when an agent comes to me for sales training, the agent will inform me that he or she is an expert or specialist in a specific product line. I will hear things like "I'm an annuity specialist" or "I'm a final-expense expert" or "I'm a Medicare Supplement specialist."

Regardless of what product line the agents feel is their specific forte, there is one thing they have in common with all the other agents. Whether they focus on Medicare Supplements, Medicare Advantage, Long-Term Care, Short-Term Care, Final Expense, Annuities or Single Premium Life, all these agents are typically working the same market. That's right; the primary market for all these agents is the senior market. They are all seeing the same people for different reasons.

The key is to understand what market you are truly in and the demographic of your typical client. By knowing that information, you can begin to lay the groundwork for a successful sales strategy.

I want you to compare selling in the senior market to playing a game of chess. There are four important things to understand about playing a game of chess. First of all, there is a board with sixty-four squares that alternate between two colors. If you have ever played checkers, it uses the exact same board. This board is your playing area or demographic for the game. The entire game will take place on this board.

So how does a chess board compare to selling in the senior market? Imagine that same chess board, but instead of having sixty-four squares, there are only twenty-six. This concept is the foundation of my twenty-six scenario sales training. Why does our game board only have twenty-six squares?

Every day you go to work, the people you meet are going to be in one of five scenarios when it comes to their health insurance. They will be on

1) original Medicare by itself,
2) original Medicare with a Medicare Supplement,
3) Medicaid
4) group insurance, or
5) Medicare Advantage.

Now that we've identified these five starting scenarios as part of our playing area or demographic, we need to identify the next set of scenarios. We know that as you encounter prospects in these five scenarios, they are going to be either healthy (insurable) or unhealthy (uninsurable). So, if we have five scenarios regarding the health insurance and the individuals in each of those five scenarios can either be healthy or unhealthy, that gives us a total of ten different scenarios.

However, we all know that everyone's lifestyle is not the same. In these ten scenarios, we will have people who are low income, people who are middle income, and people who are high income. If we apply the income scenarios, that will give us a total of thirty different scenarios.

However, we do have one small problem. We know there really isn't a scenario in which an individual who is on Medicaid has a high or middle income. That doesn't typically exist. So, when we subtract those scenarios out of the equation, it really brings us to a total of twenty-six different sales scenarios. Those twenty-six scenarios are what you as an agent run into every single day. This becomes your demographic or game board.

The next thing you need to understand is that the game of chess has pieces. There are six different types of pieces in a chess game: the queen, king, knight, bishop, rook, and pawn. Each of those pieces has specific rules that apply to its movement. For example, a rook may only move vertically and horizontally, while a bishop can only move diagonally.

In the game of selling in the senior market, we have nine pieces: the Medicare Supplement, Medicare Advantage, Nursing Home Insurance, Home Health Care, Final Expense, Hospital Indemnity, Cancer, Annuity, and Single Premium Life. Each of these pieces also has specific rules that apply to it.

The third thing you need to know about playing chess is that there are specific rules to the game. For example, two pieces cannot occupy one square simultaneously. A king and either of a player's rooks that have never been moved and have no pieces in between them may perform a move called castling.

Selling in the senior market also has rules to the game. These rules are called Medicare, Medicaid, and Social Security.

The last thing you need to know about playing chess is that there are three possible outcomes: you win, you lose, or it is a draw. Similar to selling in the senior market, you sell, don't sell, or agree to a callback.

Remember—in the game of chess there is nothing called a lead. You simply have opponents. If you lose the game, it is because you got outplayed or made a mistake.

During live training events, I always explain the concept of twenty-six scenarios. Afterward, I will ask one of the agents in the audience, "How many of those twenty-six scenarios would you like to be able to sell in?"

What do you think most agents tell me? I usually get, "Jerry I want to sell in all twenty-six!" The problem is that fifteen minutes earlier, they were totally unaware of the fact that twenty-six scenarios even existed. They had no idea of the wide range of situations they were running into, let alone how to address them properly. They probably hadn't even mapped out their market or sales process before.

Imagine the fun I get to have with an agent who hasn't heard me explain the twenty-six scenarios. I will ask that agent, "What do you think would change things for you? If you had to pick one thing, what do you think would be the difference maker for you? What would help you make more money?" The answer almost always is "That's easy! I just need more leads. If I had more leads, everything would be good. It would be all good!"

When I get that answer, I immediately reply, "Is it just a matter of having more leads, or is it a matter of having really good, qualified leads?"

Every time I say that, the agent gets a little excited and fires back almost immediately, "You're right. It's the really good, qualified leads that could totally change my career!"

At this point, I know where the conversation is going, and I will say, "So what you're telling me is that you get some responses to your marketing campaigns that are just not good leads, right? These things are just a waste of time. Do you run into that a lot? Do you run into leads that are just a waste of time?"

Almost every time, the agent will reply, "Yes, I get a ton of them. The problem is I get more of those than I do of the good leads. If I could just get more of the good leads and get rid of the bad leads, I would be just fine. I would make all kinds of money! I could be a top producer, if you could just show me how to get a bunch of those really good, qualified leads."

The problem is that I know there are twenty-six scenarios. But I also know that most agents are typically only comfortable selling in a minimum of four up to a maximum of ten sales scenarios prior to going through our training. I refer to this as the agent's "comfort zone."

This "comfort zone" is normally where agents will tell me they make the majority of their sales. When the agents tell me all they really need is just more really good, qualified leads, they are in effect telling me they aren't fluent presenters in all twenty-six sales scenarios.

What they consider to be the bad leads are actually the leads within the scenarios where they don't know how to make a presentation. They are the leads where they can't cross-sell another product because they don't understand the rules; they may not have the sales knowledge, or the products required to make a presentation in that specific scenario. These are the leads that are considered a waste of time because they don't know how to address them.

However, it is the scenarios where they understand the products, understand how to present those products, and are confident in their presentation that they consider to be the good leads.

So, we've got our good leads in one hand and our bad leads in the other, but the truth of the matter is, it isn't good leads or bad leads. It's here I know what to do and there I don't know what to do.

The key is not to make this business more difficult than it needs to be. You need to systematically work an effective process. You need to understand the demographics of your market, the pieces or the products of the game, and the rules that apply to them.

Recently, while I was conducting a live training session on final-expense sales, an agent approached me. We were talking about marketing and lead generation and he said, "You know, Jerry, here's my problem. For every ten leads I buy, about two of them are good, and eight out of the ten aren't any good."

So, I said to him, "What would you say if I could show you a way to immediately give you five times the good leads that you are getting right now? Because, if I understand you correctly, what you're telling me is that if you purchase twenty leads, only four of them on average are any good. That means that you wasted your time and money on the other sixteen. Is that correct?"

He replied, "Yes, that is exactly the problem."

I then said, "If I could do nothing but supply you with those good-quality leads, would that help you? Would you be able to do more business?"

I then took the time to explain to him how he was running into twenty-six sales scenarios. After we mapped it out, he realized he was really only comfortable selling in five of the scenarios.

I explained to him that increasing his efficiency in additional sales scenarios would require him to get outside of his comfort zone. This would require him to learn some additional products, how to present them, and a little bit more about the rules that apply to those products.

I explained to him that if he could become comfortable presenting in all twenty-six sales scenarios, the number of bad leads would virtually disappear. I asked him if he thought this information could make a difference for him. He replied, "Yes, absolutely."

All of a sudden, he looked at me and said, "Jerry, this is the best training I have ever experienced. You showed me more in the last ten minutes than I've learned in the first five years of being in the insurance business."

Remember the key to mastering the sales process is to treat it like a chess game. Remember every opponent can be beaten and every game can be won. In chess, your experience, knowledge, strategy, dedication, and the desire to win are your strengths.

These are the same strengths that will help you win in selling insurance.

MYTH 3

Cross-Selling Is Difficult

W H Y D O so many agents struggle at cross-selling? There is a very simple answer. As a matter of fact, it is so simple that it is hard to imagine agents actually struggle with it. Let's compare the process of cross-selling to a chess game. In chess, you have what is referred to as opening or beginning moves.

The first few moves in the chess opening lay the foundation for every chess game. Most of the chess openings have been named and analyzed for hundreds of years. It is important, if you want to be successful in chess, to be familiar with some of the most popular openings and understand the theory behind the moves.

Many beginning chess players ask what they should study first. While it's important to understand the concepts more than memorizing moves of a particular opening, there are a few specific openings that all chess players should start with, because they are so widely played.

For white pieces, a player should first learn the King's Gambit, Queen's Gambit, Ruy Lopez, and the English. For black pieces, a player should first learn the Sicilian Defense, French Defense, Scandinavian, and the Slav.

It's important for any chess player to figure out what type of strategy he or she likes to play. Each opening has a very different play style. Once players determine what type of game they like to play, they can then learn other openings that lead to those types of games.

This same philosophy is true for insurance agents selling in the senior market. All agents have opening moves in their presentation. These opening moves have been named and passed down from trainers to new agents for years. Here are some of the most well-known openings that new agents are often taught: "The Burial Plan," "Medicare Gaps", and "Nursing Homes Costs."

Imagine you are a chess player who only knows one opening, the King's Gambit. Your ability to beat your opponent is limited. You have to hope that your opponent is unfamiliar with the King's Gambit so that you will have an advantage in the game. The issue is that if your opponent is very skilled at playing against the King's Gambit, you may have a problem.

In a chess game, you cannot take your moves back. You cannot simply start over because you chose the wrong opening. You are stuck with the decisions you made, and those decisions will dictate whether you win or lose. The same holds true for sales presentations.

When we look back at our original question, "Why do so many agents struggle at cross-selling?" the answer is very simple. They just don't know the opening moves for a cross-selling presentation.

The problem many agents have with cross-selling revolves around the fact that the opening moves of their presentation are one-dimensional. This usually happens because the agent sets the stage to talk about one particular product from the very beginning. Again, think of this process like a chess game. Look at the openings that most agents are trained to play—openings like "The Burial Plan," "Medicare Gaps", or "Nursing Homes Costs."

For example, a Medicare Supplement agent's opening move is to say to the consumer, "Let me explain to you how Medicare works." The Final Expense agent opens with a conversation about funeral expenses or the Social Security death benefit. The Long-Term Care agent often starts a conversation discussing the high cost of nursing home care or the qualification criteria for Medicaid eligibility.

If the prospective client doesn't need or is not interested in that particular product, then the agent must either give up on the presentation or change direction; this is what we refer to as making a rotation in your presentation. This is the equivalent of standing up from the chess table and telling your opponent that you don't like how the game started and then demanding to start the game over.

This can be a difficult task for many agents. Why? Because the prospective client just watched you stand up from the table and demand to start the presentation over. From the client's perspective, the agent sounds like a used-car salesman.

Typically, this happens because what the agent says and what the consumer hears are often perceived differently. The consumer often perceives the agent as saying "If you don't need a Medicare Supplement, how about a burial policy? Oh, you don't need a burial policy? How about some nursing home insurance?"

The problem is that an opening based on creating a need for multiple product solutions was never established. When the agent ran into a dead end on the initial presentation, he had to establish a new presentation flow, or in other words start all over.

There is a very simple solution for this problem. You need to learn a new set of opening moves for your presentation. It is no different from learning a new opening for a chess game. The opening I want to share with you I refer to as the "Combo."

The theory behind the "Combo" is to start the presentation in a way that creates a discussion on multiple product solutions without requiring a rotation in the presentation. It is important to remember that these opening moves must set the stage for the presentation from the very beginning.

The "Combo" opening I am going to teach you is designed to provide you with a template for achieving three distinct advantages: control, momentum, and power.

Let's start by talking about control. In chess, the objective is to take control of the center of the board. Why? Because the most coveted vantage point on the chess board is the center of the board. Think of it as a strategic hill where you gain advantage over the enemy by being comfortably perched there and just shooting down at them. If you gain control of the center, you gain control of the game.

From the center, you can attack very quickly and conveniently to any side. You can easily maneuver pieces from the center to any point on the board. If you remain concentrated on one particular side of the board, it will be hard to quickly maneuver to the other side in case of emergencies.

The center of your presentation is the place that gives you the ability to present Medicare Supplements, Medicare Advantage, Final Expense, Hospital Indemnity, Cancer, Single Premium Life, Annuities, and Nursing Home Insurance, using only one presentation format. You must control the center.

The key to controlling the center is based upon your opening moves and understanding the theory behind those moves. Begin with identifying what all these products have in common. The common thread with each of these products is that they are all commonly considered to be senior-market products. Therefore, the key is to find topics important to seniors that will allow you to have a conversation that will encompass all the products. Then you must convert those topics into a single presentation theme or, in other words, your center of the board.

Now let's look at some topics that relate to each of those products. Medicare has changes annually in deductibles and copays, which in turn affect Medicare Supplement policies.

Medicare payments based on the prospective payment system have impacted the utilization of nursing homes for short-term recuperative stays. This has created a need for Home Health Care, Short-Term Care, and Long-Term Care policies.

Shortfalls in Medicare Part C could expose a person to thousands of dollars in out-of-pocket expenses. This is especially true for critical illnesses. These shortfalls can be addressed by using cancer, critical illness, and hospital indemnity policies.

Social Security has a limited benefit for funeral expenses. Typically, Social Security is discussed when presenting final expense or single premium life insurance as a solution for funeral expenses.

Social Security Survivors Insurance has limited benefits for the surviving spouse. Social Security income will be lost with the death of a spouse. In addition, those benefits may be taxable. Annuities, single premium life, and final expense policies are often used to address income replacement and tax issues for surviving spouses.

Many people who enter a nursing home may ultimately have to depend on Medicaid benefits, especially if they do not carry any Long-Term Care or Short-Term Care insurance. However, qualifying for benefits is based on the income and assets of the applicant.

This requires a person to use his or her income and assets first to cover the cost of care, prior to Medicaid eligibility. Often, a Long-Term care policy or a Life Insurance policy with living benefits, along with a Short-Term Care insurance policy, can provide a better solution than relying on Medicaid.

It would appear that all these products can be covered in one discussion about Medicare, Medicaid, and Social Security. Often, agents make the mistake of setting the stage or utilizing an opening for their presentation based on only one of these topics.

For example, the Medicare Supplement agent wants to explain Medicare, the final-expense agent wants to discuss the Social Security death benefit, and the agent discussing nursing home benefits wants to explain Medicaid eligibility.

In order to present multiple product solutions and increase your cross-selling opportunities, the presentation needs to include Medicare, Medicaid, and Social Security.

Remember the center of the board in your presentation is based on controlling the conversation on the topics of Medicare, Medicaid, and Social Security. Control the conversation on those topics, and you have control of the presentation.

Now, let's discuss creating momentum. This is where our opening moves come in. The objective of opening with the "Combo" is to provide you with the momentum required to capture or control the center of the board.

To accomplish this in a chess game, we would attempt to gain an advantage over our opponent by controlling the direction of the game. This is the same technique you want to use in your presentation process.

How can you accomplish this every time? What is the opening move? The first move of the Combo opening is to get the prospective client to ask you to discuss Medicare, Medicaid, and Social Security with them. I repeat, get *them* to ask *you*!

Never start a presentation until the prospective client asks you to do so. Often, agents make the mistake of starting a conversation by telling the prospective client that they are going to explain what is covered by Medicare, Social Security, or Medicaid. Then they will whip out a pad of paper or some other form of presentation material and start a presentation. Worse yet, they rely on a strictly verbal conversation, without the use of any third-party information as verification that what they are stating is actually true.

Why is this so important? If you start a presentation without the prospective client asking you to show them the information, it will be viewed as a sales pitch. If they *ask* you to explain the material to them, it will be viewed as an educational process.

Setting the stage to discuss Medicare, Medicaid, and Social Security and getting prospective clients to ask you to discuss those three topics with them is relatively easy. This is the next move in the Combo opening.

What I want you to do is stop telling people what is covered by Medicare, Medicaid, or Social Security, and focus on a mentality of discussing what is *not* covered.

Try using the following example. "Mr. and Mrs. Jones, what most people tell me is that they get inundated with information from all over the place on what Medicare does, what Medicaid does, or what Social Security does. However, what most people share with me is that their real concern is what is *not* taken care of between Medicare, Medicaid, and Social Security. Has anyone ever *really* explained to you what is not taken care of between those three governmental programs?" The key here is to stress the word "really" in a way that creates doubt.

Their response typically will be *no* or *not really*. Respond by saying, "Would you like me to do that for you?" The prospective client will generally respond by saying yes or something equivalent.

You have now set the stage for your presentation, and most importantly, the prospective client asked you to explain or present the facts. Getting the prospective client to ask you for the facts eliminates the problem of your presentation being viewed as a sales pitch. Instead, they will perceive it as an educational process.

Your opening moves have now given you the momentum to assume control of the center of the board in your presentation.

Now that you control the center of the board in your presentation, you need to understand the power that it gives you. In sales, the most powerful tool is information. By controlling the presentation process, you have the power to gain the valuable facts and insights as to the prospective client's concerns, fears, and beliefs.

When you know their beliefs and you can show them a way to overcome their concerns and fears, you have created a very powerful presentation. With that type of presentation, you should win far more often than you lose.

All you have to do is simply change the opening moves for your presentation.

MYTH 4

Fact-Finding Is Easy

THROUGH THE YEARS, I have trained numerous agents in the field. Often, I would ride with experienced agents who were struggling. The hope was that I could help elevate their sales performance. There were always three things these experienced agents would typically say to me at the end of the day.

The first thing was that they could not believe how everyone was just spilling their guts to me. It was amazing how the people were just telling me everything.

The second thing was that they could not believe how everyone that day just wanted to buy something.

The third thing was that I had to be one of the luckiest guys in the world. Everything that day just fell into place. Any agent who showed up at the door could have sold the deal. They would proclaim that they never get that lucky, and they did everything exactly the same way that I did it.

Well, maybe they were right and I am one of the luckiest guys in the world, because my lucky streak has continued for over thirty years. If you ask my wife, she would agree with them. She always tells me I am lucky to have such a wonderful and understanding wife.

I agree with her on that point, because she has put up with my passion and obsession with insurance and has been incredibly supportive throughout the journey.

However, I don't believe that those other agents implemented a sales process identical to mine. What those agents did not understand was that it is the little things, not the big things, that make a difference. It was the little things that happened right in front of them that they did not even notice that made the difference in my presentation.

The key is having the ability to get people to tell you things they did not even realize they told you. I would have people ask me all the time, "How did you know that?" You will know when you have actually started to master the art of fact-finding because people will ask you that same question.

To begin, we know that Medicare, Medicaid, and Social Security have limitations, coverage gaps, and eligibility criteria regarding hospital expenses, medical expenses, prescription drug expenses, death benefits, survivor's benefits, and nursing home expenses.

I have found through more than thirty years of training agents that utilizing a presentation format that starts by discussing Medicare, then moves to Social Security, and ends with Medicaid has had the best results and creates the most logical flow in the consumer's mind.

It is important for you, as an agent, not to look at this process as a presentation. This is the process of educating the prospective client. The goal during this process is to discover the prospective client's concerns, fears, and needs, while educating them about the potential financial pitfalls associated with these programs.

It is very important to remember that at this point, you are not offering solutions; you are just gathering the facts. Mastering this process will enable you to gather all the facts needed to understand the client's entire situation so that you can determine the appropriate product solution or combination of product solutions you are ultimately going to present.

Agents often tell me they have no problem gathering the facts. I ask them if they have any difficulty making the decision regarding which product or products they will ultimately present to the prospective client. They typically will respond by saying, "No, that part is easy." Hopefully, that would not be your answer.

The reason I say that is because there is one important piece of the math that you need to understand. Remember: the more facts you gather, the more needs you will discover, and the product solutions you can present will multiply.

Therefore, if you believe that deciding on what product or combination of products you are going to present is easy, it probably means you already had that decision made before you met the prospective client. It also means you do not put a lot of effort into the fact-finding process.

Remember gathering facts is an art. Many agents today feel this is the easiest part of the sales process. They will say they don't need to learn anything about gathering the facts. Some will say they have this awesome form they created with all these fields on it for gathering information.

They may feel like it is easy, but in reality, how often do these forms get used? We all know it can make a prospective client feel uncomfortable when you whip out a three-page financial survey or fact finder and start quizzing them on the spot. Why is that? It is because it appears intrusive and feels like a sales pitch. People start to become uncomfortable with the process when you start writing things down. These are the very same reasons agents give me for why they don't use a fact finder worksheet.

When an agent asks a direct question, it is often perceived by the prospective client as being too forward or intrusive. If you've ever had a prospect tell you that something was personal or that it was none of your business—or even "I don't know" when they clearly did—this would indicate that you asked a direct question and got a direct *negative* response. What you should have realized after the fact was that the question should have been asked a different way.

It is important to learn how to use indirect questions versus direct questions. So, let's talk about how you can avoid being viewed as intrusive by utilizing indirect questions. First, let's talk about what kind of questions would be considered indirect questions.

Indirect questions are those that provide you with the information you are looking for without directly asking for that specific information. It is that simple.

I have always trained agents to gather facts by utilizing three separate questioning methods. The first method is direct general questions. The second method is indirect questions. The third method is direct questions that you do not want the prospective client to answer. This is what I refer to as window questions.

Now, I know that sounds a little strange. Why would you ask a question you do not want them to answer? With window questions, you are looking through the question and immediately, with a very slight pause, asking another question in lieu of the first question, before the prospective client has the opportunity to answer the original question.

Think of it like a magician's trick. In my right hand, I'm holding a shiny red ball above my head, and while you are focused on my right hand, I reach into my pocket with my left hand and pull out a blue ball. Now, we all know that at one point I am going to switch that red ball to the blue ball.

Here is an example of a window question: "Mr. Jones, just like you, people will often ask me about nursing home insurance. The truth of the matter is that most people don't actually need it. So, before we waste any time discussing it, we should evaluate your ability to pay for a nursing home without any insurance.

"Now, I know earlier you told me that the only income you have is about $3,200 monthly between your Social Security and pension. Technically, that income could help pay part of the nursing home bill. So, you already have a big part of the bill covered."

"Mr. Jones, it is important to remember that if you enter a nursing home, you are no longer trying to make your estate bigger. Instead, you're just trying to keep it from getting smaller. Most people have investments that they don't take an income on. Usually, these accounts just accumulate, but in all fairness, that income could also help pay some more of the nursing home bill. Do you have any accounts like that?"

This is a direct general question. If he says yes, I am going to follow up with an additional question, my window question.

"Mr. Jones, how much a month could the income from those accounts help pay toward the nursing home bill?"

Now, I know he doesn't get a monthly income; therefore, the answer would require some calculation on his behalf. This question is like that red ball in my right hand. Before he gives me an answer, because I don't want him to, I will ask the next question.

"Mr. Jones, to make it simpler, if the accounts were earning 3 percent interest, how much a year could we count on from those accounts to help pay toward your nursing home bill?" The second question is easier to answer and requires less calculation.

Let's just say he answered about $6,000. Here is what just happened. He told me that he has roughly $200,000 invested somewhere, accumulating growth. Most importantly, I now know where the money for my presentation will come from. In addition, I will not have to reduce his monthly income to solve the problem, because I will reposition those unallocated earnings.

Then I would say something like "Well, I'm sure you're earning at least 3 percent, or you wouldn't have your money there, right?" I would wait for his response. For now, let's just say he agreed. I would reply, "The good thing is that gives us another $500 a month toward the nursing home bill."

Now, I have gotten him to reconfirm that $6,000 a year is at his disposal. I can easily base my presentation on repositioning that unallocated income in a way that will solve his problem.

Asking the right questions is important, but not asking the wrong questions is even more important. What do we mean by wrong questions? These are the questions that when answered have a negative impact on your presentation.

Here is an example. The prospective client tells the agent they have a Medicare Supplement and that they had a minor surgery a couple of years ago. The agent then asks them how things went on the bills. First of all, Medicare Supplements all participate in Medicare crossover claims filing. Therefore, the insured obviously did not have a problem filing the claim. Secondly, most Medicare Supplement plans would typically pay the majority of out-of-pocket expenses.

Therefore, the agent can only get a positive response from the client regarding their current company. So, hats off to that agent, who just got the prospective client to state that their current insurance is great!

Even if the agent said he could save the prospective client some money with lower premiums, the agent has already implied that some companies can be difficult to collect from. This happened when the agent asked about their claims experience. This creates a situation where the prospective clients feel that there may be a risk to saving money and decides to stay with their current carrier.

You should think of your questions as falling into one of four different categories. The first category would be qualifying questions. These are the questions where you discover information about their health, financial, or family circumstances that either qualifies or disqualifies them for certain product solutions.

The second category is funneling questions. These are the questions that are used to gather more detailed facts and refine the picture of the prospective client's circumstances. Here is an example: "Martha, you told me that your daughter lives locally. Is your daughter a stay-at-home mom, or is her family a two-income family?"

The third category is adhering questions. These are the ones where the prospective client's answers draw them to the presentation. These questions address problems related to the presentation.

Here is an example: "Martha, you told me earlier that your daughter and your son-in-law both work. If your daughter were to lose her job, do you think it would have a negative financial impact on her family?" If she replies yes, I would then say, "So if your daughter had to quit her job to take care of you, you're saying that it would have a negative financial impact on her family. Is that correct?"

The fourth category is elevating questions. These are questions that can tie them to the big picture. For example: "Martha, if you were to have a serious illness, there are four likely outcomes. You could receive care at home, in the hospital, in a nursing home, or you might end up in a funeral home. Out of those four places, which one do you want your kids to have to pay for?"

Most importantly, regardless of what kind of questions you are asking, you need to listen. Do not assume answers. The stereotypical salesperson talks too much and fails to listen. If that's how you sell, you're missing out on significant opportunities.

Throughout the sales process, prospective clients will drop clues as to what they're thinking and how they're feeling about you and your products or services. In other words, they're telling you what they like or dislike, what they fear, and what their biggest concerns are.

This is precisely the information you need for determining what product solutions you will present and for closing the sale. The crazy thing is they're giving it to you. All you have to do is focus on listening! Selling is 100 percent about listening. If you are not a good listener, you'll have to work a lot harder to make the sale.

There is one last piece of advice that I have for you regarding the fact-finding process. When you develop your process, follow through with that process from the beginning to the end every single time. Often, agents develop what I refer to as the "dinner bell syndrome."

Imagine a cat that is trained to stop what she is doing and immediately run to her food bowl every time she hears the dinner bell. What the agent does is stop the fact-finding process and immediately go into a product presentation as soon as he or she sees the first opportunity. Avoid the dinner bell syndrome. If you don't, you will never be an effective cross seller. You won't master selling multiple products simultaneously or increase your income.

MYTH 5

Warm Up and Then Jump into the Presentation

T H E   E M P H A S I S   on presenting the solution as fast as possible leaves little time to understand the unique nature of the customer's situation. In fact, the standard approach assumes that the customer has completed some sort of self-diagnosis and therefore will be able to connect your solution to the problem.

Jumping into the presentation too quickly will usually end with a negative outcome. So why and how does this happen? It is easy for an agent to get caught up in the details of a product. But your potential customers aren't necessarily interested in your product. They are typically interested in what your product will do for them. How will it solve their problems? How will it help them achieve their goals? How will it save them money? How will it protect them from risks?

Getting caught up in product details is usually what causes an agent to jump into the presentation too quickly. It also tends to lead into the practice of rushing through the presentation. Make sure you always translate your product's features into your customers' benefits. Don't focus on the bells and whistles; instead, focus on how those features can solve problems for the client.

You know by now that selling insurance is very similar to playing chess. Keep in mind that before you play a game of chess, you must first prepare the board. All the pieces must be organized and placed on the appropriate starting squares. Prepare for your presentation just as you would a game of chess. Two problems that can significantly affect an agent's success are failing to organize and lack of mental preparation. If you do not organize the board, you cannot play the game. If you are not mentally prepared for the game, you will lose.

There are four objectives you want to focus on prior to and during your presentation. These will help you avoid the urge of jumping into or delivering your presentation too quickly.

Understanding, organizing, and implementing a strategy for these objectives is the way you need to prepare for starting and delivering your presentation.

1) Slow the tempo.
2) Create an educational environment.
3) Create elevated credibility.
4) Project a professional image.

Let's start with our first objective: "slow the tempo." This refers to the speed of speaking that the agent uses during the presentation and the speed at which the agent moves through the presentation. Often during a presentation, the agent unknowingly speeds up how fast he or she is talking or how quickly the agent moves through the presentation. This can happen not only with new agents but with agents who have years of experience. With new agents, it is usually because they are anxious. With experienced agents, it is because they are out of rhythm. I don't care how good or talented you are as a salesperson; you will always have those days when you can't get into rhythm.

How do you combat this problem? You must create a mental trigger that will help you find your rhythm. It is all about slowing down and hitting your presentation stride. Whenever I played in a chess tournament, I utilized a mental trigger to help prepare me for each game. Before each game, I would sit down across from my opponent and stare at the board without saying a word. Then I would stand up, reach across the table, introduce myself, and shake their hand with the utmost confidence. I would envision that I had just won the game and was congratulating them on a game well played. I wanted to remember that feeling of victory before the game started. I wanted to be mentally prepared for beating my opponent.

I would watch their reaction to my pregame ritual. My goal was not only to find my rhythm but to analyze their pregame demeanor. If they appeared to be even slightly intimidated or unsure of themselves, I would start the pace of my opening game with a faster sequence of moves. I wanted them to feel as if it would require little effort for me to beat them. I wanted them to believe I could think much quicker and had more experience. I wanted them to think about that handshake and how confident I seemed. When playing chess, taking control of your opponent's mental perception is a strategic tool. This is also true for conducting a sales presentation.

One of the best examples I can give you was my first state chess tournament in high school. There are four people on a team, and as a freshman, I took the spot of one of the seniors. The other players were all friends and seemed unsure about this new young kid bumping their friend off the team. But that was the coach's call.

During a pivotal match, I made a terrible move that caused me to lose my queen, the most valuable piece on the board. If you lose your queen while playing against a high-caliber player, the game is typically over. I realized at that point that I no longer had the power on the board to beat my opponent and that I would have to beat him off the board.

After losing my queen, I made the next move very quickly, as if I gave it little thought. I put my head in my hands and projected a defeated and disgruntled demeanor. As my opponent made each move, I would again make a move with the appearance that it was sporadic and not thought through.

My opponent believed the game was in hand. It was only a matter of time before he would shake my hand in victory. I could tell that my teammates were second-guessing the fact that I was even on the team.

As my seemingly sporadic moves continued, my opponent's focus started to diminish. After all, as far as he was concerned, this game was already over. All of a sudden, I stood up from the table and reached my hand out to him. With a smile, he stood up to shake my hand and accept my resignation. However, just as he started to extend his hand, I made one last move and declared victory.

He stood there in total disbelief. How did this happen? The other players on his team could not believe what had just happened. What my opponent failed to realize is that even though he had control of the board by controlling the pace of play, I was able to set a trap and walk him straight into it.

When I started selling insurance, I wanted to develop a technique like the handshakes before my chess matches, to prepare myself mentally. I wanted to remind myself of the speaking speed and rhythm of my presentation. This technique enabled me to prepare mentally for the pace of the presentation. I have taught this simple technique to numerous agents throughout the years. I am going to share it with you, and I hope it will help you as much as it has me.

First, I want you to think about vacuuming a floor. If you have ever used a vacuum cleaner, you have probably at some point stretched the cord too far and accidentally unplugged it. The vacuum cleaner will go from making that loud sweeping noise to a fading sound that diminishes to nothing. I want you to envision the sound that the vacuum makes when it gets unplugged, how the sound winds down to silence. Think about the speed of your presentation and the pace of your speaking and bring it down as if it was a vacuum cleaner that became unplugged. Your presentation should not be based upon the sound of the vacuum while it is running, but rather on the silence after it is unplugged.

Before every presentation, I would think about that vacuum coming unplugged from the wall and adjust my mental pace for the presentation.

Our second objective is to: "create an educational environment."

There is a big difference between educating someone and pitching someone. Make sure you involve the prospect in this process. Empathy is the real secret to success in sales. You need to have the desire to understand and relate to your customers' wants, needs, challenges, and problems so you can help them in the best possible way. Often, starting the presentation too quickly can cause the prospective client to become defensive and anticipate that the sales pitch is coming. You should always properly set the stage for the presentation from the very beginning.

I told you this earlier, but it is critical that you do not start the presentation until the prospective client asks you to. Remember—when they ask you to present them with information, it creates an educational environment. Starting the presentation without them asking will create the perception of a sales pitch.

Creating an educational environment with the prospective client will put them at ease with the process. It creates presentation collateral, and it will be viewed as educational material instead of a being part of a scripted sales pitch. The educational process not only educates the prospective client regarding the need for your products but helps educate you on their needs.

Remember selling is not about telling! Selling is about being a problem solver. In order to be a true problem solver, you need to shut up and let your ears do the work. You have to listen for the problems and identify them before you can solve them.

Imagine if you had an appointment with a doctor, and the doctor immediately summed up what was wrong with you simply by looking at you as you walked through the door. The doctor then recommended surgery for your illness without an examination. How would you feel? If you present a solution to your customers without digging deep into the challenges they are facing, you are doing exactly what that doctor did. You're prescribing a solution before diagnosing the problem. Don't present a solution until you're sure what the problem is. Remember to educate prospective clients instead of pitching them.

Our third objective is to: "establish elevated credibility." Establishing credibility is an important part of the sales process. In live training sessions, I have one segment that is devoted to creating credibility. During that segment, I ask agents three questions. The first question is "What are elements of credibility?" They often suggest things like a proven track record, a list of satisfied customers, number of years in business, business size, etc.

My next question is "How do you establish that credibility or convey that credibility to a prospective customer?" Invariably, the response is "I tell them."

Now the tough question: "How different is your credibility story from that of your biggest competitors?"

Unfortunately, other than a few minor elements, they are likely to sound quite similar. Therefore, their credibility story suggests that they are more equal to their competitors than different.

This type of credibility is what I refer to as "assumed credibility." In other words, people assume that you wouldn't be in business if you couldn't provide this level of credibility. They really see it as being legitimate instead of credible. A legitimate insurance agent is one who is legally licensed to sell insurance. A credible insurance agent is one who is honest, knowledgeable, experienced, and trustworthy. This is what I refer to as "elevated credibility." This type of credibility elevates your image so that prospective clients view you as a trustworthy expert.

To truly set you and your company apart, what needs to be developed with your potential customer is this elevated credibility. Assumed credibility is what you know about your business and your product solutions. Elevated credibility is based on what you know about your customers. It is your ability to relate to their circumstances, recognize their problems, and offer solutions. You want them to understand that this is not the first time you have heard their story.

Often, when I would meet with potential clients, I would analyze their circumstances, diagnose their problems, and offer a solution like it was child's play. They would look at me with amazement and comment on my ability to take their complex issues and solve them as if they were trivial.

I would tell them that there was a reason why I could come up with a solution for their situation so quickly. I would explain to them that many people in the industry think I am some kind of sales guru. When companies ask me to be a guest speaker at a meeting, I have agents approach me and ask how I became so knowledgeable. They would ask how they could become like me.

I would then look potential clients in the eyes and say, "Here is the truth to the matter. I am not some kind of genius or guru. I am not some great salesperson. I am simply an intelligent man with years of experience. If you spend your entire life from the age of nineteen listening to the stories and problems of people that are over the age of sixty-five, it gives you quite an education. These were people that had all experienced problems that I had never faced. When you learn to listen and help them find solutions for their problems and put yourself in their shoes, it gives you an entirely different perspective."

"In reality, as much as I would like to say that I am great at what I do, the truth is that I have already seen your exact situation of being a couple with a son who can't handle money, two daughters, and a granddaughter who has a drug issue, numerous times."

"I have already met your family numerous times through the years. I addressed your concerns and solved your problems before we ever met. At this point in my career, it would be extremely rare for me to run into circumstances that I have not already seen. The only thing I can actually provide you with that someone else can't is access to my knowledge and experience, because without that, I am just like everyone else."

The best way to develop elevated credibility is through diligent preparation and thought-provoking questions that demonstrate your experience. Unfortunately, most salespeople prepare very little, ask too few questions, and seldom reach the required level of asking thought-provoking questions.

Now that we have discussed how to create elevated credibility, let's look at how agents self-destruct their own credibility. The main way agents destroy their own credibility is lack of organization.

Unorganized presentations and the lack of ability to produce the required forms are large contributors. Secure and check your collateral material, including applications, brochures, rate sheets, and the like. They form the basis of what you are selling.

Agents often find themselves in a situation where they do not have the forms they need to fully complete the application process. If agents find themselves digging through their sales kit looking for forms or sales aids while in front of the client, they lose credibility.

Remember people want to deal with professional, credible people who are successful. Lack of organization makes you appear unprofessional and unsuccessful.

I'm sure you'll agree that establishing credibility is one of the most critical elements in securing a new customer. The customer must see you as a credible and trustworthy resource. Do not self-destruct your own credibility by appearing disorganized. You want to project a professional image.

This brings us to our fourth objective of: "projecting a professional image." When I refer to projecting a professional image, it links back to that "assumed credibility" we discussed earlier. It is the image of success and trustworthiness. It is your brand.

Projecting a professional image is all about addressing two distinct problems. The first one is obvious. We want to enhance our assumed credibility, to increase our ability to close new clients. Secondly, we want to utilize our professional image as a tool to combat buyer's remorse.

That's right—a tool to combat buyer's remorse. You see, most agents think of their professional image only on the level of selling new business. They fail to utilize their image to *retain* business. If your average commission per sale is $700 and you get twenty people a year who decide to cancel because of buyer's remorse, that is $14,000 per year. Now, if you tell me you don't get twenty people a year who suffer from buyer's remorse, then you simply are not working to your maximum potential. If you are really out there shaking the trees, you will have at least twenty.

However, if you could reduce the number who actually canceled from twenty to ten just by improving your professional image, wouldn't it be worth it? When agents invest in their professional image, the budget is based on a mentality of getting new business, which equates to a small budget. This happens because agents feel they can talk their way around the cracks in their image.

Their belief is that it is better to spend the money on lead generation. So, they try to replace the $14,000 with new sales instead of investing any money to keep it from leaving in the first place. Let's look at the math this way: If you can save half of the cases, that would equate to $7,000, right? So, if I could show you a way you could spend an extra $1,500 a year that would save that $7,000, would that make sense to you? That is a 700 percent return on your investment.

Keep in mind that I am not pitching you to join JLS Sales Academy. I am talking about five very inexpensive ways to invest in your professional image.

Number one is your business card. When it comes to marketing tools, the business card is about the most versatile. This is obvious because the business card is your potential client's first exposure to the products and services you or your company has to offer. Therefore, the design of your business card fills an important purpose in the success of your company.

In today's world, potential clients are always concerned about your legitimacy and your credibility. If you are a con artist or running a scam, what is the one thing you are not going to give someone? You would not want to give them a way to identify you. Make an investment in a professional photographer and put your picture on the front of your business card. This will help show your potential clients that you are legitimate and credible. By doing this, your card becomes more of a credibility tool instead of merely an advertising piece and will help greatly reduce buyer's remorse.

Number two is a vanity email address. This is another important item for building your credibility. Keep in mind that successful businesses usually do not have Gmail, Hotmail, or Yahoo email addresses. A vanity email address makes your business look larger and improves your credibility. It shows your customers that you are serious about your business. Every time you give out your email address, you are advertising your business.

Number three is client engagement or welcome letters. Why is sending an engagement or welcome letter a good idea? Often, when a consumer purchases a new insurance policy, it may take several weeks before they receive it. Clients can become anxious and may start to question their decision.

An engagement or welcome letter lets the client know that action has been taken on their behalf. It gives you the ability to reaffirm your commitment to providing quality service to the client. It also gives you the ability to reaffirm your credibility and a larger professional image in their mind. Large companies have a process in place for new clients; small companies generally do not.

Whether you are selling a $500,000 annuity or a small final-expense policy, how you set and manage your client's expectations can make a huge difference in your client's experience during this process. Managing these expectations will help you build a relationship with that client that will have long-term effects on your agency's bottom line. Clients who have unrealistic expectations from the beginning are more likely to be disappointed and cancel.

It is your job as their agent to set realistic expectations and manage those expectations throughout the application process. Expectations that become a problem often revolve around the time frame of the application process. These expectations should be addressed in your client welcome letter.

The client welcome letter should include information about you, your firm, important timelines, what the client should expect from you, and what you will expect from them. The client welcome letter should be mailed to the client within the first few days after they fill out an application.

Number four is branded new client folders. Printed materials are an excellent way to establish your brand. Companies of all sizes need to be concerned about perception. It forges a connection between the buyer and the seller. It communicates superiority and competitive differentiation. It enables the agent to stand out among all the others.

Let's talk specifically about professionally branded client folders. Why use them? First of all, it is more professional and helps keep the client's paperwork organized. Again, it projects an image of credibility and size. It differentiates you from other agents and helps the client recognize that you are a business aside from the actual insurance company.

Most importantly, it helps alleviate buyer's remorse. Often, an agent makes a sale, and that evening, the client experiences buyer's remorse, resulting in a cancellation call the following morning. This often happens when the client is looking at the insurance company brochure that the agent left on the table earlier that day, depicting a nursing home confinement, getting sick, or dying. It can also happen when the client looks at a consumer's guide left by the agent that reflects caution.

A bunch of loose paperwork on the table begs the client to pick it up and look through it again. However, the problem is that you are not there to address any concerns they may have or any confusion regarding what they read. Not to mention other people coming to visit, like a family member, friend, or neighbor; information left out in plain view often begs for the input or opinion of a third party. These people were not there for your presentation. Therefore, their input is not based on knowledge or facts but purely on their opinion of the issue or product.

This is why new client folders are important. You can organize all the material regarding the transaction inside the folder. When the client looks at the table that evening, they see an attractive folder that exudes the credibility, size, and service of your business instead of the insurance company's brochure, receipt, or consumer's guide. It makes the transaction seem complete and organized.

If a family member, friend, or neighbor stops by later that day, the details of the transaction are not laying out in open sight. They would have to pick up the folder and open it in order to view the contents. This would be considered intrusive and an invasion of privacy by most people. If it did happen, your client may be offended by this intrusion and less likely to listen to their input.

If utilizing branded pocket folders eliminates buyer's remorse and conserves just one sale a year, then more than likely, you covered the cost of the folders. There are numerous ways you can improve your professional image at very little cost.

MYTH 6

Presentation Materials Are for Amateurs

EXPERIENCED AGENTS often tell me that they do not need presentation materials. Often, they will point to their head and say, "Jerry, it's all up here. I don't need any crutches!" All throughout my career, I have always used presentation materials, because these materials gave me third-party credibility. I could show that it wasn't just my opinions; it was the facts. I wasn't asking people to take me at my word. They didn't have to agree or disagree with me; they had to agree or disagree with the rest of the world. After all, I was just the mediator.

I can't tell you how many times I have said to a prospective client, "I completely understand your position. The tough thing for me is believing that all these credible sources including government agencies are completely wrong. Do you think it might be possible that they have access to information that is unavailable to you that substantiated their position?"

If they replied yes, I would respond, "I have access to the information they used to substantiate their position. Would you like me to share it with you?"

This is a great way to regain control of an argumentative prospect. Remember getting the prospective client to ask you to educate them puts you in total control of the presentation process.

These materials are simply tools that are used to build your presentation. If you were a construction worker, would you go to work with only part of your tools? Imagine a person who needs reading glasses. He wants to read the menu at a restaurant, but it is difficult. Sure, he might be able to make out a few items, but most of the menu is unclear. He has three choices: he can order something that he assumes is on the menu, he can ask the waiter about the specials, or he can ask the waiter for a pair of reading glasses.

Trying to make a presentation without third-party verification material is like trying to read that menu without reading glasses. Why do it? So why do so many agents do it? The answer is actually very simple. It all boils down to one thing: they are afraid of looking like a salesperson.

Agents will go to great lengths to avoid the appearance that they are salespeople. I will give you a few examples.

There are some commonly taught methods for making the initial contact with a prospect at the door that I find absolutely comical. Many of these commonly taught methods actually hinder the agent's ability to close or retain business. Let's take a look at a few of them.

When agents go to the door, their biggest concern is often looking like a salesperson. They try to avoid it at all costs. I often have agents tell me that they go to the door carrying nothing or a clipboard. Others tell me that they leave their car running while going up to the door. That one really cracks me up.

The bottom line is that just because you go to the door without your tools or you leave your car running does not mean that the consumer is going to invite you in. It doesn't improve your chances.

Typically, regardless of the circumstances, you will have to talk your way into the house anyway. Leaving your car running or leaving your sales material in the car has no real positioning value. It can actually hurt your presentation flow.

The agents who employ these tactics are trying very hard to avoid looking like a salesperson, but why? When the consumer looks out the window or answers the door, what are these agents trying to imply? Are they looking for directions? Are they a meter reader? Does any of this really make a difference? Sure, going to the door with a large briefcase could be intimidating. People might wonder what you have in it. For all they know, maybe there is a gun in it. Maybe, you are going to rob them. Today, people are always concerned about letting people in their homes. I would rather open the door to a salesperson than a robber.

At one point, you must tell the truth, and the truth is that you are a salesperson. Why are agents so concerned about this? Because they are trying to avoid one question: "Are you selling something?" Unfortunately, these same agents tend to answer that question by saying no or something equivalent. This typically comes back to haunt them later when the prospect says, "I thought you said that you weren't selling anything." There is nothing worse than backtracking in an attempt to repair the damage you have done to your own credibility.

Let's talk about what happens if the prospect opens the door; you converse with them for a moment, and they invite you in. Agents immediately want to walk in at this point. They don't want to break the momentum they've created by going back to their car for sales materials. However, once inside, if they only carried the clipboard or pad of paper in with them, they have to find a reason to go back out to their car at some point, so they can retrieve their sales tools.

This creates a potentially huge disconnection point during their presentation. They can lose the momentum. It provides the prospect with a way out of their presentation. What happens if the prospect says that there is no need for you to go to your car and that they are short on time anyway?

It is simply six one way and a half a dozen the other. You either carry your tools to the door to begin with or try to find the perfect time to go back out and get them later. The issues you face are the same, regardless of the timing. The only difference is that one takes place at the door and the other takes place inside the house, but the problem is still the same.

PRESENTATION MATERIALS ARE FOR AMATEURS

That is why other agents will leave their car running. That way, when they get invited in, they can say they need a moment to turn off their car. This gives them the opportunity to grab their sales kit. Those are the sneaky agents who think they are actually fooling someone.

What they think is happening and what is going on are two different things. Think about it like this: their primary goal was to avoid looking like a salesperson at the door. However, if they succeeded at this during their first encounter, it creates another problem. When they leave to turn their car off, it creates a second contact point, and this time, when they reach the door, they definitely look like a salesperson. The problem here is that the prospect may feel intimidated when the agent returns with sales material in hand, regardless of what the agent told them the first time.

The important thing to remember is that you do not want to deceive the consumer with what you say, how you present yourself, or your actions. My mother always told me that there are two types of people you should not trust. She would say, "Believe in people and trust everyone right up to the point that they do not trust you." She would remind me that untrustworthy people do not trust other people. She also told me never to trust a person who pretends to be something he's not. I have found these to be very valuable words of wisdom.

However, I don't suppose these beliefs were unique to my mother. I would say that they are universal, the internal core belief of all trustworthy people. I personally would never trust an insurance agent who came to the door with a clipboard or left their car running. I have found through years of training agents that these agents often lack a moral compass. However, sometimes they were just following the instruction of someone else.

So, if you are an agent who works this way, I am going to give you the benefit of the doubt and go with the belief that you have just been following the advice of someone else.

There is an advantage to carrying your collateral material with you to the door, in addition to a perceived disadvantage at the same time. The question is, how can you have the best of both worlds?

Here is what I would recommend: Use one of those leather three-ring portfolios as the sales kit for all your collateral materials. However, you need to make sure that it has a shoulder strap. When you go to the door, carry your sales kit over your shoulder. At the door, tuck it slightly behind your back so that both of your hands are free. This is the least intimidating and most effective way to approach a prospective client's door.

Your sales collateral is less noticeable and not quite as intimidating to prospects. Most importantly, it is with you, and you are prepared to enter the prospective client's home. You are not pretending to be anything different from what you are. You are not creating any possible disconnection points at the door or in the house.

I cannot overstate the importance of having the right tools for the job. It's all about positioning, credibility, and capitalizing on the moment. Often, the small details inadvertently undermine an agent's credibility. However, there is another component in becoming a master presenter.

Look at any professional athlete and ask yourself, "What makes them special?" It is because they can consistently replicate a specific action. For example, the professional golfer can hit a golf ball very consistently. The professional baseball player can hit a baseball very consistently. Their consistency is what makes them professional. It is their ability to swing at the ball the exact same way every single time and get consistent results.

Printed presentation materials give you a road map for consistency. A structured presentation can help keep you on track. If the presentation inadvertently gets off track, it gives you an easy way to pick up where you left off. A structured presentation along with its collateral material is not a crutch. It is more like a golf club or a baseball bat. It is the tool you use to consistently swing at the ball and deliver the perfect presentation every single time.

Your sales presentation should have a good, clear framework for your message. Not only does the right structure help you efficiently get from point A to point B. It is important to simplify your message: without a clear and consistent structure, a presentation can seem more complex than it is. A good structure takes your audience down a path that leads to a natural and obvious conclusion.

In the world of sales, structured presentation materials are for professionals. It is only amateurs who don't use them.

MYTH 7

Great Salespeople Can Wing It

PREPARATION IS the first step toward an effective sales presentation. Preparation doesn't necessarily mean that you practice it until you have it memorized. You don't want your presentation to sound too rehearsed. It should have a natural but structured flow to it. Having a well-rehearsed and structured presentation will make you and the client feel more comfortable.

Unfortunately, preparation is a discipline that seems to be fading in the routines of many salespeople. The world is full of insurance agents who either have little respect for their customers' time, no particular interest in doing their jobs well, or an overinflated view of their own ad-libbing abilities. Any of these situations can produce a sense that the agent doesn't need to prepare and that on the spur of the moment, he or she will come up with the most persuasive things to say, in the most effective manner.

An agent once asked me to give him the CliffsNotes version of my sales training. I told him to have an answer for every question and a story for every objection. Be focused, disciplined, and deliver a consistent, well-constructed presentation every single time. In other words, "Do not wing it."

You must have a plan. Many salespeople work without a plan—reactively and opportunistically going through month after month without a strategy. Just because you have a plan, that doesn't mean you'll always follow it. But if you don't have a road map, how do you expect to get where you want to go?

You need to be disciplined. Succeeding in sales is incredibly difficult. Often, it's not even fun—the daily grind, the activity required to get through the prospecting process in order to find the sales. It not only is a ton of work but requires daily discipline to stay focused and actively on the path to success. Look at the most successful insurance agents, and you'll find men and women who get up early and do what it takes every day to make their numbers.

Learning is the foundation of sales success. Having a continuous focus on product training, sales training, and studying the changes within the market are crucial. Often agents who believe they are great salespeople do not focus on learning anything new. After all, they are already great; what could they possibly learn that they don't already know?

You must adapt. The way you were taught to sell ten years ago might not be as effective today. The tools you used, the approach that once worked might fall flat today. You must be able to adapt to the changing market and the changing customer if you want to avoid declining results. Successful insurance agents constantly adapt their strategy and execution to what's changing and working around them.

Remember one thing: "Great salespeople do not wing it." They are disciplined, focused, and have a plan. Their presentations are well constructed, concise, and consistent. It is the agents who are legends in their own minds who often make a habit of winging it.

MYTH 8

Don't Present Multiple Products Simultaneously

THIS IS a very complex myth and probably one of the most well known throughout the insurance industry. In order to begin tackling this myth, we must look at the difference between cross-selling and upselling. The confusion between the two is where the roots of this myth began.

Cross-selling generally occurs when the insurance agent has more than one type of product to offer consumers that might be beneficial to them. An example of this would be selling a Medicare Supplement policy along with a short-term nursing home policy.

Upselling differs somewhat from cross-selling in that the insurance agent is concerned not with selling an additional product to generate additional commissions but with selling a higher-end version of the same product. For example, selling a life insurance policy with a $25,000 face amount rather than a $10,000 face amount.

One of the main differences between upselling and cross-selling is in the approach that the salesperson takes when engaging in either method. When cross-selling, the agent identifies an additional need that the customer has and fulfills that need by recommending an additional product.

Upselling is often less needs based and more value based. It involves the agent painting a picture of "more is better than less." In other words, "more" has a better value.

In many ways, cross-selling and upselling are similar, in that they each offer customers additional value over what they would have otherwise received had they only bought what they were initially looking for.

A successful cross-selling and upselling agent will be able to paint a picture of the value that the customer will receive so that the customer will be able to visualize the benefits of making the purchase. Upselling provides higher quality, and cross-selling provides additional quality.

The ironic part is that most of the agents who believe in this myth believe that you should upsell. In their minds, there is a huge difference between upselling and cross-selling products simultaneously. Typically, that is why these agents are not good cross sellers. You see, they believe that if you are going to cross-sell, it should take place at a different time.

For example, if you are going to sell a Medicare Supplement, talk about short-term nursing home coverage when you deliver the policy. These agents believe that talking about multiple products will confuse the customer.

The problem is that the presentation on delivery never seems to happen. Because now they are afraid that if they try to sell more, it might jeopardize the first sale.

However, this same agent would think nothing of telling someone they should improve their benefits by replacing their Plan N Medicare Supplement with a Plan G Medicare Supplement. It would increase the premium but provide a better value.

This myth is based on believing you can upsell on the same appointment but that you can't cross-sell on the same appointment. Is this because the consumer will get confused, or is it because the agent will get confused? Is there really a difference? If an agent suggests to someone that they should buy a $25,000 face amount instead of $10,000 so that their surviving spouse can pay the funeral expenses and receive additional funds for income replacement, it is considered an upsell because it is only one policy providing higher benefits.

However, if an agent suggests to a person buying a Medicare Supplement that they should have the comprehensive nursing home benefit instead of just the basic coverage, it is considered a cross-sell because it requires a second policy providing additional benefits.

In both situations the concept was to solve two problems. The only difference was that one situation required one policy while the other required two.

The theory behind the myth is that simultaneously presenting multiple policies or products complicates the presentation and confuses the consumer. Whereas upselling does not. However, if we look back to our first myth, "You have to be great at selling your product," we know that we are not really selling multiple products; we are selling one concept that requires multiple product solutions.

You solve a problem by selling a product. You solve multiple problems by selling a concept. Do you think consumers get more excited about solving one problem or multiple problems? I can tell you from experience that it is easier to make a sale solving two problems versus one. I can also tell you that it is easier to make a sale solving three problems instead of two.

MYTH 9

Lead Generation Is Difficult

L E A D   G E N E R A T I O N is all about creating a funnel. Let's start by going over the basics of what most salespeople consider to be a sales funnel. First, salespeople will utilize a little terminology to describe the funnel. They will say that there are three types of people you'll interact with during the sales process: leads, prospects, and customers.

A lead is considered to be someone who becomes aware of your company or someone you decide to pursue for a sale, even if they don't know about your company yet. Typically, this includes everyone in one big group, but you could also break this down further to only look at qualified leads, which are leads that meet certain qualifications to become customers. For example, if you're selling Medicare Supplement products, a qualified lead is someone age sixty-five-plus.

Prospect is a term that is used interchangeably with *qualified lead,* but usually, a prospect is someone who has had some kind of contact with your company. For example, they sent in a reply card from your direct-mail campaign requesting information.

We all know what customers are! These are people who have made a purchase. All these people fit into your sales funnel.

To envision a sales funnel, think of an inverted pyramid or the shape of a kitchen funnel. Here's an example of a sales funnel. At the very top of the funnel, you have leads. This is where you cast a wide net, trying to find as many leads as possible to bring into the sales funnel. In the middle of the sales funnel is the reduced percentage of those leads that become prospects, people who are actually interested in your product or service and who are qualified to buy. The bottom of the sales funnel is the customer, the small percentage of people who are interested in your product and who will actually make a purchase and become a customer. It's a numbers game. The more leads you bring into the sales funnel, the more prospects you'll have. This is important, because the more prospects you have, the more customers you have.

So now you know how most salespeople generally describe a sales funnel. The problem is that loading a sales funnel of leads and prospects to ultimately gain a client is typically an expensive and slow process. I use a different terminology for that process. I would refer to that type of funnel as prospecting funnels, not sales funnels.

So, what is a sales funnel? A sales funnel is a system of providing appointments where you get paid to run them. Your sales funnel is making you money, not costing you money. In addition, the average commission is over $40,000 per case, and the closing ratio is over 90 percent.

Trust me; I am not pulling your leg. Recently, during a live training, I had an agent make the remark that "the numbers appeared to be an incredibly high benchmark." He asked what those numbers were based on. I told him it was based on my personal sales funnel during the last five years I spent in the field.

He asked me what it took to build that kind of sales funnel. I responded, "In order to build that kind of sales funnel, you need to change your mentality and some of the terminology. Instead of putting leads into the top of the funnel, change those leads into existing clients."

Instead of funneling "leads" down to "prospects," change that terminology to funneling "existing clients" to "qualified appointments." Qualified appointments are the existing clients who want an appointment with you. However, in this situation, these clients have already provided you with the details of their assets, income, family dynamics, needs, and concerns prior to the appointment. In addition, the client already knows why you are coming, and you already know that they have hundreds of thousands of dollars in movable liquid assets.

I then chuckled and said to him, "If an agent has that type of qualified appointments and can't close 90 percent of them or can't average over forty thousand in commission per sale, there is a problem."

So now that I have explained my definition of a sales funnel, let's take a closer look at how I created it.

Let's start by looking at the top of the funnel, which is filled with existing clients. These clients were put into the funnel by other agents. I refer to these agents as the "sales agents." These were the agents I had hired and trained to sell Medicare Supplements, final expense, hospital indemnities, short-term care and other typical senior market products. I created a lead funnel for all them utilizing direct mail and other lead-generation methods.

Each time the sales agent makes a sale, he or she informs the client that their policy will come in a customized organizational binder. The agent will inform the client that the binders are not a boilerplate product and that each binder's index tabs were designed specifically for their unique situation.

The agent will then proceed to fill out an index-tab worksheet based on the type of assets the people own. These worksheets are the initial fact finder. However, clients do not perceive them as intrusive because they are simply providing the information needed to construct their personal binder.

These agents are paid 50 percent of the total agency commission for obtaining the initial sale. In order to keep these sales agents focused on selling, I do not have them deliver their policies. Instead, this task is handled by another set of agents. These are referred to as the "delivery agents."

The delivery agents have a higher skill set and knowledge base. Not only can these agents sell the typical senior-market products; they are also well versed in Long-Term Care insurance, Annuities, and Single Premium Life.

The delivery agents work by appointment only. Their job is to deliver the policies along with the binders and pick up all the money that was left on the table by the first agent. These delivery agents already have an overview of the client's assets, based upon the index tabs in the binder. By offering to construct or fill the client's binder during the appointment, they are able to get all the assets on the table.

When the delivery agent sells additional business, the original sales agent is compensated with a referral fee that equals 12.5 percent of the total agency commission. This enables the sales agent to make thousands of dollars in additional income each year.

The delivery agents would then receive 50 percent of the net agency commission, which was calculated by subtracting out referral fees paid to the sales agent.

As the delivery agents worked through this process, they would find clients who were referred to as the elephants. The problem with the elephants is that these clients are time-consuming and often require dealing with existing competition. The sales process for these clients often takes months, with numerous visits.

The delivery agent's job is to create the need for an overall plan and gather all the pertinent facts while setting the stage for my introduction.

By taking over the clients who were considered to be the elephants, I was able to free up the delivery agents' time and enable them to complete more policy-delivery appointments.

This was my sales funnel of existing customers who wanted an appointment with me. These clients had already provided me, through the delivery agent, all the details regarding their assets, income, family dynamics, needs, and desires before the appointment. In addition, this client already knew the purpose of my visit, so the stage had already been set, and I knew that they had hundreds of thousands of dollars in movable liquid assets.

The commissions generated from these clients were still divided in the same manner. The sales agent received 12.5 percent of the agency commissions, and the delivery agent received 50 percent of the agency net commission.

Even though my sales funnel may seem complicated, you can easily duplicate it. Consider yourself to be the sales agent, just as you do now, and fill the top of your funnel with leads. Then utilize the binder concept on all your sales. When the policies come in, put on a different hat, and now you're the delivery agent. Approach that delivery as a new lead and follow through with the sales process. I promise you, you will double or triple your income. All it takes is learning some new products along with the techniques in presenting those products and access to proven industry knowledge and sales training.

You will make a lot of money as a sales agent, but the real money will be made as a delivery agent. As a delivery agent, you only work by appointment, and you don't have a lead cost.

MYTH 10

Closing the Sale Is Difficult

THERE IS a reason that it's referred to as the "art" of closing. In order to master the process of closing the sale, you need to avoid certain mistakes.

One common mistake made by agents is relying on some sort of natural talent or perceived personal skill to close the sale. In reality, closing the sale is more like a chess game than a talent or beauty contest. Strategy and knowledge win every time. Obviously, gaining the knowledge necessary to strategically close sales requires confident individuals committed to learning and then implementing what they learn in their sales process.

There are three simple things that you can do to simplify the closing process. The first is to formulate a plan for dealing with objections. Remember each objection you overcome gets you closer to the sale.

Often, an agent's sales plan is based on hoping to avoid certain objections, instead of learning how to overcome or even preemptively address them. The best way to deal with an objection is to negate it before it even arises.

If you track the objections you receive and work on creating a response to them, you can incorporate those responses into your presentation before they even come up. That being said, you will always get some level of objection or pushback from clients. This is just part of the process. Do not view these moments as a negative or address them in an adversarial tone. If you do, it may cost you the sale.

Instead, try congratulating the prospect for being so astute or even acknowledging and agreeing with the objection. Use that opportunity to make sure you understand specifically what they are objecting to and drill down to find out whether it's a true objection or not.

Try phrases like "So let me be sure I understand your question" or "I think I understand where you are coming from, but just to be sure, you're saying that (objection X) is what you are really concerned about, right?"

The second thing you can do to simplify the closing process is changing the response you are looking for. One big mistake that can make closing the sale tough is looking for the yes. Agents often sit back and wait for the prospective client to give them a yes.

In effect, they want the client to say, "Yes, I want to buy the policy. Go ahead and write it up!" As agents wait for that magical yes, they continue to provide reasons as to why the consumer should buy. They talk about the policy features themselves or the company, all while sitting there waiting and waiting for the yes. This is referred to as "talking through the close."

Let's face it: people usually fear making decisions. This is because they are afraid of making a wrong or bad decision. Therefore, it is perfectly natural that a prospective client would be apprehensive about saying yes. However, if the client doesn't say yes in this situation, the agent does not make a sale. The key here is to look not for the yes but for the no.

To avoid this situation, you need to start *assuming the sale* instead of trying to close it. By assuming the sale, you are putting yourself into the strongest possible selling position. This is where looking for the no comes in.

Instead of requiring the prospective client to say, "Yes, I want you to write up the application," assume the sale and make them say no if they have an objection. Remember—if you are looking for the yes and the client doesn't say it, you did not make a sale.

If you are looking for the no and the client doesn't say it, you made the sale! Even if they do say no, it will typically come with some explanation or objection. This gives you the opportunity to address the problem.

Assuming the sale begins by having a positive attitude, enthusiasm, and confidence in yourself and your abilities. You need to have a thorough knowledge of the product or service you are selling and the belief that it will benefit your client. You need to have a heartfelt desire to help your prospective client that exceeds your desire to earn money for making the sale.

The third thing that will simplify the closing process is your ability to understand what your job actually is. What do I mean by that? Many people have a fear of making a decision, especially a bad decision. It is your job to reassure them that the decision they are about to make is the correct decision. They want you to reaffirm the decision and allow them to feel good about it. It is that simple!

JUST A THOUGHT

In Conclusion

NOW THAT we have tackled those ten sales myths to-
gether, I want to take just a moment and say thank you. I have
appreciated the time we have shared, even though it was not
in person. I hope you did also.

Hopefully, you were able to get at least one nugget of information that inspires you. There is so much more that I would
love to share.

I would like to ask one favor of you. As you go about your daily
routine, I want you to remember something that I spoke about
earlier in this book. It is a truth so profound that I don't want
you to forget it. Instead, I want you to think about it every day.

"The most difficult hurdles to overcome are the self-imposed
limitations that we place upon ourselves."

If you believe in yourself and you believe you can accomplish anything, you will succeed. I know I believe in you, and I hope that someday I will have the privilege of meeting you in person and listening to your story of success.

ABOUT JLS SALES ACADEMY

JLS SALES ACADEMY was developed with a philosophy of providing every insurance agent in the senior market with the knowledge and tools that can empower them.

Our goal is simple: We want to help you become the best you can be. We want to help maximize your potential.

In today's competitive environment, the need for sales training and support is greater than ever. Whether you are an individual agent, agency manager, or an insurance company, we have programs that can simplify the process of receiving or providing sales training.

The JLS Sales Academy platform can be accessed seven days a week and twenty-four hours a day. The platform contains hundreds of instructional sales videos and an entire library of collateral material.

The agency management portal provides detailed information regarding the progress of each sub-agent participating in the program. This gives agencies the ability to track and manage their sales training.

The JLS Thrive program gives the agent that next-level experience. With this program, we provide a more personal hands-on approach, enhancing the agent's sales training experience.

For more information on JLS Sales Academy,
visit www.JLSSalesAcademy.com.